BOOK OF

Garlic

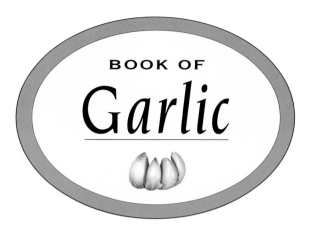

BOOK OF

Garlic

JACKIE FRENCH

Angus&Robertson
An imprint of HarperCollins*Publishers*

An Angus & Robertson Publication

Angus&Robertson, an imprint of
HarperCollins*Publishers*
25 Ryde Road, Pymble, Sydney NSW 2073, Australia
31 View Road, Glenfield, Auckland 10, New Zealand
Distributed in the US by HarperCollins*Publishers*
10 East 53rd Street, New York NY 10022, USA

First published in Australia in 1994

No Library of Congress Cataloging Publication Data
available at the time of printing.

ISBN 0 207 18545 X.

Printed in Hong Kong
9 8 7 6 5 4 3 2 1
97 96 95 94

CONTENTS

GARLIC

History of Garlic

Here it is recorded how much black radish, red onion and garlic went to the workers.

~

HERODOTUS, GREEK HISTORIAN

Garlic (*Allium sativum*) might be described as a pungent, bulbous, cultivated perennial — but this definition in no way gives even a hint of the magic and allure of garlic.

Like many people, my early years were spent garlic-less. My love affair with garlic started in my early 20s, when former peasant dishes came to be considered high cuisine, and a widening interest in herbal remedies brought back a lot of the lore of our great-grandparents. This seems to have been the fate of garlic — to be alternately loved and abandoned — for thousands of years.

Garlic is traditionally a peasant spice and remedy. In Ancient Egypt it was fed to labourers building the pyramids to give them strength (and possibly to increase their resistance to waterborne diseases). It was

Hot Garlic Sauce

This is excellent with roast lamb, beef, chicken or fish, or steamed vegetables.

~ *1½ tbspns spring onions (scallions)*
~ *6 garlic cloves, chopped*
~ *3 tbspns olive oil*
~ *1 red capsicum (sweet pepper), finely chopped*
~ *1 tomato, peeled and diced*
~ *1 bay leaf*
~ *3 cups (750 ml/1¼ imp pt) stock (beef, chicken, fish — it depends on what the sauce will be served with)*
~ *1 tspn fresh tarragon, thyme or coriander, finely chopped*

Fry the spring onions and garlic in the oil until the spring onions are tender. Don't brown. Add all the remaining ingredients except the fresh herb. Simmer for 10 minutes, remove from the heat and stir in the fresh herb.

If you want a richer sauce, whisk in 1 tbspn butter as soon as you take the sauce off the heat.

used as an offering to the Ancient Egyptian gods (garlic cloves were found in Tutankhamen's tomb, dating from around 1352 BC), and Egyptian husbands of the same era were said to chew garlic on the way home from their mistresses so their wives would not suspect that they had been engaged in amorous dalliance.

Ancient Roman and Greek warriors ate garlic for strength and courage, and it was an important part of the stores of Greek military triremes. In Greece athletes chewed garlic before the Olympic Games to give them endurance (while lovers ate it to give them endurance of another kind). The Romans applied a plaster of crushed garlic to cure haemorrhoids.

There is a Muslim legend that when Satan stepped out of the Garden of Eden, garlic sprang up under his left foot. The prophet Mohammed is said to have advised that garlic be applied to the bite of vipers or the sting of scorpions, and in many parts

*This is wonderful with
grilled or broiled chicken,
cold ham or roast pork.*

~ *6 tbspns olive oil*
~ *10 garlic cloves, crushed*
~ *1 kg (2 lb) ripe tomatoes,
skinned and quartered*
~ *2 tspns ground almonds*
~ *juice of 2 oranges
(preferably bitter Seville
oranges)*
~ *½ tspn orange zest
(no white at all), grated
(shredded)*

*Heat oil and sauté the garlic
until soft. Throw in the
tomatoes with the garlic.
Simmer for 10 minutes or
until quite thick. Add the
almonds and juice, bring to
the boil again, then take off
the heat at once before the
sauce gets bitter. Stir in the
orange zest.*

of the world it is still applied to relieve the effect of
venom. It was held to be a sacred herb (known as
'moly') with magic healing properties by
European gypsies.

Garlic was not so well regarded, however, in
some aristocratic circles. The Roman patrician
Virgil recommended it as a food for labourers, to
give them strength for the harvest. The priestess
Medea is said to have smeared her lover Jason
(a hero of Ancient Greece) with garlic to repel her
father's savage bulls. Presumably they were
aristocratic bulls, not enamoured of peasant smells.

In 1368, King Alphonso of Castile instituted a
new Order of knights — one of the rules being that
any member who had eaten garlic should not come
into the King's presence for a month.

Garlic originated — and still grows wild — in
Central Asia around Uzbekistan, Turkmenistan and
Kazakhstan, in the Altai Mountains of Siberia, and
in the Ural Mountains near the Caspian Sea. (Italian
chefs, however, may insist that it originated in
Sicily, and occasionally Indian cooks will claim
it as theirs too.)

Garlic has been domesticated in China for at least 5000 years, in the Middle East for at least 4000 years, and it is mentioned in the earliest Indian Vedic writings. The Romans brought garlic to much of northern Europe, and Columbus, reversing the trend of taking New World plants back to the Old World, took garlic to what is now the Dominican Republic. From there, the eating of garlic spread across Central and South America.

Garlic has a similarly long medical history. The Codex Exelser, an Egyptian medical papyrus from about 1500 BC, lists 22 garlic remedies for heart problems, worms, and as a general tonic. According to Pliny, the Ancient Eygptians used garlic to repel scorpions and serpents, and he and Dioscorides valued it as a treatment for asthma, worms, and as a tonic and diuretic.

In the Middle Ages, garlic was esteemed as a cure for leprosy and deafness (it may, in fact, have helped skin conditions that resembled leprosy and also some hearing problems). It was believed that garlic

Garlic Toast

SERVES 1

~ *2 slices coarse white bread*

~ *2 garlic cloves*

~ *3 tbspns olive oil*

~ *cheese*

~ *tomatoes*

Toast the bread until it is golden-brown. While still very hot, rub the cut clove of garlic over it, dribble on a little olive oil and top with slices of cheese and tomato.

This is also very good with anchovies and tomatoes.

'neutralised foul air' and so prevented pestilence. Medieval doctors wore masks stuffed with garlic to protect them from the plague, and during the Great Plague in the 17th century, garlic cost more than its weight in gold in London. Garlic was one of the ingredients in Four Thieves Vinegar, used by Marseilles grave-robbers during the 1722 plague to give them resistance to infection from the corpses they robbed. The 17th century farrier, Gervase Markham, fed horses that suffered from nightmares with balls of garlic, liquorice and aniseed.

In Victorian England, bruised garlic cloves were applied to the chests of consumptive children, or bound to the feet to ease inflammation of the brain. Even as late as World War I, garlic juice was still applied to wounds as an antiseptic by the British Army (and probably quite effective it was too).

WHY GARLIC STINKS

*We absolutely forbid it entrance to our Salleting, by reason of its intolerable
Rankness. To be sure, 'tis not for Ladies' Palates, nor those who court them ...*

~

EVELYN ACETARIA, A DISCOURSE OF SALLETS, 1699

It is mostly the sulphur compounds in garlic that make it smell — and
most of these are found in the pale yellow garlic oil, which makes up
about one-tenth of the weight of the clove. The most important of these
is alliin, which is odourless, but which is converted to allicin, one of
the main active ingredients in garlic, making up to 0.4 per cent
of the clove. Allicin smells.

Garlic's aroma is excreted via the lungs and skin — which is why
your breath and sweat may smell of garlic.

*This traditional Italian
dish is usually brought to the
table in a large pottery dish
and placed over a small
spirit lamp to keep it warm.
The diners then dip raw
vegetables in it: pieces of
asparagus or cardoon, strips
of capsicum (sweet pepper),
very young parsley, fresh
broad (fava) beans, slices of
firm tomato, strips of peeled
and seeded cucumber, or the
white part of spring onions
(scallions).*

~ *4 garlic cloves*

~ *6 anchovies*

~ *1 cup (250 ml/8 fl oz)
olive oil*

*Mix the ingredients in
a blender (liquidiser).
Alternatively, crush the
garlic and anchovies together
and add the oil drop by drop.
This makes a thicker, richer
mixture. Pour into a serving
dish and keep warm at the
table. (In some recipes a little
butter is also stirred into the
warm mixture.)*

HOW TO STOP GARLIC SMELLING

An old gardening tradition asserts that garlic is
sweeter and less pungent when grown in warm
climates. In cold areas it will be bitter and biting.
This, however, may have more to do with the local
varieties grown than with climate. And according
to Medieval lore, if garlic is both planted and
harvested when the moon is below the horizon,
it will be far less pungent. I haven't tried it.

How to Stop Your Breath Smelling

Eat a few sprigs of fresh parsley (chew well). Nibble a slice of raw
ginger. Or chomp on a few fresh mint leaves. I was told by a French
friend that good red wine would also remove the smell of garlic
(or at least change it into a more acceptable perfume). It didn't — but
the experiment was fun.

It has also been claimed that eating lots of garlic reduces the smell —
that it is only the person who eats the occasional bit of garlic who gets
smelly breath. This is a remedy for garlic addicts.

It is mostly raw garlic in salads or semi-raw garlic in garlic bread,
however, that flavours the breath. Cooked garlic is much sweeter and
less pungent. Perhaps the final remedy is to simply encourage everyone
to eat a lot of garlic so that no one notices the odour anymore.

How to Stop Your Hands Smelling

Scrub garlicky hands with salt in cold water and lemon juice, then
wash with warm, soapy water. Alternatively, place ½ cup (60 g/2 oz) of
bicarbonate of soda (baking soda) in a blender (liquidiser) with the juice
of 2 lemons and a bunch of parsley. Blend thoroughly. Keep in a jar in
the refrigerator and dip your fingers in it after peeling garlic.
Wash with cold then warm soapy water.

Garlic Butter

SERVES 4

This delicious butter is ideal for frying prawns (shrimps), tomatoes, mushrooms, scallops, fish or green leafy vegetables. Dab a little on steamed carrots, potatoes, asparagus or lobster, or spread it over hot bread.

~ *500 g (1 lb) butter (preferably unsalted)*

~ *2 tspns fresh parsley, roughly chopped*

~ *6 garlic cloves*

~ *1 little black pepper (optional)*

~ *a squeeze of lemon juice (optional)*

Blend all ingredients or pound them together in a mortar — or just chop very finely and whip together.

Garlic butter can be wrapped in greaseproof (wax) paper or a freezer bag and frozen. Rounds of frozen garlic butter will slice neatly.

HOW TO STOP YOUR REFRIGERATOR SMELLING

Never leave garlic or an uncovered dish of garlic sauce in the refrigerator. However, for when accidents do happen — sprinkle a few drops of vanilla essence (extract) over a little jar of bicarbonate of soda (baking soda) and leave it open on a shelf.

WHICH GARLIC?

We recall the fish which we did eat in Egypt for nought, the cucumbers,
and the melons, and the leeks, and the onions and the garlic.

~

HOLY BIBLE, NUMBERS 11: 5

Cloved Garlic (Allium sativum*)*

There are too many varieties and cultivars of *Allium sativum*, or cloved
garlic, to list here. They range from large white varieties through to
small red to purple to creamy-yellow ones. Small cloved varieties
include Californian early and late, Mexican purple, Italian purple and
South Australian white. Large cloved varieties include giant Russian,
New Zealand purple and Glenlarge. The latter is a modern 'day-length
neutral', early-maturing cultivar (can be planted at any time of year).

Elephant Garlic (Allium ampeloprasum *and* A. giganteum*)*

There are two types of elephant garlic — or Aï d'Orient or Oriental
garlic, to give it its old-fashioned name — *A. ampeloprasum* and
A. giganteum, not *A. sativum*. Both types of elephant garlic look more
like leeks than garlic when they are growing, although it is the bulbs
rather than the leaves that are mostly used. They have very large
bulbs with proportionately enormous cloves, but a much milder

Grilled Garlic

~ sprigs of rosemary
~ garlic cloves
~ olive oil

Pull the leaves off the rosemary twigs. Peel the garlic and thread the cloves on the twigs. Brush with olive oil and grill. You really need an outdoor grill for this — grilled garlic is really too pungent for a kitchen. It also needs smoke and the scent of grilled meat to come into its own.

Jumping Garlic

~ garlic cloves
~ olive oil

Brush the peeled garlic cloves with oil and drop onto a very hot barbecue plate after the meat has been barbecued and the plate is covered with fat and meat juices and charred bits. The garlic will sizzle and jump around, absorbing these remnants. Scoop the cloves up when they are just beginning to brown and serve with the meat. They might just help mitigate some of the effects of the barbecue.

flavour than *A. sativum. A. ampeloprasum* grows about one-third taller than *A. sativum* — usually to almost 1 m (3 ft) high but often taller in good soil. It has more leaves than normal garlic, though the number of leaves of both can vary according to growing conditions; the flowers are pale pink to pale green.

A. giganteum is even bigger, growing to over 1 m (3 ft), with pale lilac flowers and much wider leaves than either *A. sativum* or *A. ampeloprasum*. Its leaves are covered with a faint white 'bloom'.

Other 'Garlics'

Garlic chives (*Allium tuberosum*) are hardy, flat chives that are deliciously garlic-flavoured. Society garlic (*Tulbaghia violacea*) has garlic-scented leaves, as have ramson (*Allium ursinum*), which is a shade-loving, groundcover herb.

Garlic chives

GROWING GARLIC

Garlic will grow almost anywhere — but in some places you will have to work harder to get a good garlic crop than in others. Garlic does best in a climate of cool winters and hot summers, with lots of sunlight, in rich but very well drained soil.

To grow garlic, you need to plant garlic cloves. Usually, the bigger the clove, the better start the plant has and the more garlic it will produce — though small cloves will give big bulbs in good soil. This is one of the reasons why garlic is relatively expensive. Unlike lettuce, where one plant produces enough seed for hectares or acres of new lettuces, you will need to keep about one-tenth of your garlic crop to plant again next year (to allow for wastage etc.).

Plant the garlic cloves about 10 cm (4 in) apart, with the pointed end upwards (if you plant them pointing downwards,they will possibly still grow), in fertile, well-drained soil. It is preferable for the soil to be slightly alkaline, although garlic still grows well in quite acid soil. One old-fashioned method was to dust the cloves with wood ash. This protected the cloves from being eaten by beetles and other soil-dwelling insects until they had sprouted. It may also have helped to make the soil slightly alkaline and to inhibit disease.

Garlic can be planted at any time of the year except midwinter, but to get the best bulbs, the garlic needs to be chilled below 10°C (50°F). If the bulbs aren't chilled early on in their growth, you will get smaller, uneven cloves, and the bulbs may

Whole Garlic in Vine Leaves

SERVES 4

~ 12 garlic cloves
~ 12 small, young, tender grape leaves
~ 6 tbspns olive oil
~ juice of 2 lemons or limes

Wrap each garlic clove neatly in a leaf. If necessary, secure with toothpicks. With practice, you may be able to make a neat parcel that won't unravel.

Place the parcels at the bottom of an ovenproof dish. Pour the oil and juice over them, then put the lid on. Bake in a slow oven (150°C/ 300°F/Gas Mark 2) for 2–3 hours.

The vine leaves can be served warm or left to cool.

Oven-cooked Potato Chips with Garlic

SERVES 4

~ 4 potatoes

~ 8 garlic cloves

~ 3 tbspns olive oil

Peel the potatoes and cut into chips. Peel the garlic. Place both in the bottom of a baking dish (pan) and sprinkle a generous amount of oil over the top. Bake in a hot oven until browned, stirring every 20 minutes or so. Serve hot.

not last as long because they will have thinner or less papery skin.

In warm temperate areas, where winter temperatures fall below 10°C (50°F) but the ground does not freeze, plant garlic in autumn (fall). In areas where the ground freezes solid throughout winter (not just for a few hours after a heavy frost), plant garlic in spring, as it may rot in frozen soil, particularly if it's damp. In cool temperate to hot areas, chill cloves for a month in the refrigerator before planting. In hot areas, plant in midwinter, when the ground has cooled down and you can be sure that it won't warm up again until spring. Even though garlic is mostly a cool-climate crop, you can still get a reasonable amount of home-grown garlic in hot regions — as long as you remember to chill the cloves and plant them at the right time.

Whatever the time of year that the garlic is planted, it will be maturing as the days lengthen. This is necessary to get the best sized bulbs — garlic will be small if it matures in cold weather.

As the garlic grows, the original single clove fills out, becoming fatter and rounder, and then dividing into six to ten, or sometimes more, new paper-covered cloves. (Of course, if the soil is poor or the garlic is crowded or badly fed, you may only get three or four small cloves.)

Your first sight of the growing garlic will be dull green leaf tips that develop into long, flat leaves.

By late spring, the stalk will emerge — round, thick and a slightly paler green. This can grow to 1 m (3 ft) or more, though it's usually about half that size. This stalk finally flowers. Garlic flowers can be spectacular — bright blue, pale purple, pale pink or a creamy, greeny white. In very cool climates, garlic may not flower at all and will simply die back as the days get shorter and colder. The flower eventually dies and the stalk begins to wither. This is when you pick your garlic.

FEEDING GARLIC

Garlic needs to be fed — the better it's fed, the bigger your bulb will be. As a rule of thumb, spread a little poultry manure or blood and bone over the soil when you plant your cloves, then feed them again when the young leaves begin to grow rapidly in spring. The young leaves can also be mulched with compost, old leaves, lucerne or alfalfa, or clover hay — in fact any good mulch will do. Take care, however, NEVER to dig the mulch into the soil near the garlic cloves. Let it sit on the surface to be drawn into the soil naturally by worms and other soil life. Undigested organic matter in the soil may breed pests and diseases — and leave you with a rotting or nibbled crop.

Garlic Soup with Cheese

SERVES 4

~ 6 cups (1.5 l/2½ imp pt) beef, chicken or fish stock
~ 15 garlic cloves, chopped
~ a few sprigs of fresh thyme or tarragon
~ bread, sliced and fried in olive oil
~ cheese, grated (shredded)

Simmer the stock, garlic and herb for 10 minutes. Place a slice of bread scattered with cheese in each soup bowl. Strain the stock and pour it hot over the bread and cheese. Serve at once.

Ramson

Chicken and Garlic Soup

SERVES 4

Excellent for cold winter's nights — or if you're sniffling with a cold.

~ 6 cups (1.5 l/2½ imp pt) chicken stock

~ 10 garlic cloves

~ juice of 2 lemons or limes

Simmer stock and garlic for 10 minutes. Strain, then stir in the lemon juice (make sure it is free of pips, which might make the soup bitter). Serve at once.

SAVING GARLIC FOR NEXT YEAR'S CROP

You need to save about one-tenth of your garlic to grow the same amount next year. Choose good, big cloves. If possible, save individual cloves, not the whole bulbs. Though garlic is ostensibly 'cloned' and every bulb should be the same, in practice there is some gradual mutation, and the more varied your selection, the more genetic diversity you'll have.

Some varieties of garlic produce what look like miniature bulbs or 'rounds' on top of the plant. These are not seeds — they are top-borne cloves. If you plant them you will get a small, round garlic clove at the end of the next growing season. If you leave them in for another year's growth, you will get a large garlic bulb again with small 'rounds' on top.

Garlic plants that have propagatable cloves on both the top and bottom of the plant have a good survival mechanism. If you can find any of these old-fashioned varieties, cherish them —they are often hardier than new cultivars, with a sweetness or nuttiness that commercial cultivars may lack.

Problems with Garlic

Small Cloves

One of the major problems with home-grown garlic is small cloves. This is caused either by growing a small-cloved variety, by not feeding your garlic enough, or by lack of chilling.

Some garlic varieties are much larger than others, but most garlic cloves, whatever the variety, need lengthening days to form large bulbs. In other words, they need to be planted in autumn (or in early spring in areas where the ground freezes) so that they mature with the season. Some modern cultivars, however, are 'day-length neutral' — they can be planted at any time of the year.

Weevils

Various garlic weevils may attack, either when the plant is in the ground or has been harvested. Keeping the soil clean of undecomposed organic matter will usually stop soil weevils from invading your bulbs while they are still growing (mulch the surface of the soil, where earthworms can draw it under naturally instead of digging it in).

Tomatoes with Garlic and Cream

This dish can be incredibly rich and fragrant — as long as the tomatoes are sweet, red and softly ripe.

~ *1 tbspn butter or oil*
~ *6 garlic cloves, chopped*
~ *8 ripe tomatoes, skinned and sliced thickly*
~ *½ cup (125 ml/4 fl oz) (single/light) cream*

Heat the butter or oil and fry the garlic until soft. Don't brown or burn. Slide the tomato slices into the pan and fry quickly until the juices just start to run, then remove the tomatoes. Add the cream and bubble quickly until it thickens. Return the tomatoes to the sauce, reheat and serve at once.

Aïoli or Garlic Mayonnaise

~ 4 garlic cloves
~ 1 egg yolk
~ 1 cup (250 ml/8 fl oz) olive oil
~ 1½ tbspns lemon juice

Place the garlic in a mortar with the egg yolk and crush until they are perfectly blended. (This can be done in a blender (liquidiser), or even with the back of a spoon if you don't have a mortar and pestle.) Now take a fork and dribble in, drop by drop, half the olive oil, beating well all the time. This is a slow process — don't try to hurry it. Now add half the lemon juice, drop by drop, then the remaining oil, whisking all the time, and finally, the rest of the lemon juice. The result should be rich and shiny — almost ropey.

If you want a creamier dressing, add 2–4 tspns tepid water, again drop by drop, and beat well. Dijon mustard or salt and pepper can be added to taste, but aïoli is much more pungent than mayonnaise and shouldn't need it.

Traditionally, garlic tops were braided into garlands to stop weevils attacking the bulbs once they'd been harvested. Rigorous cleanliness will also prevent weevils — never store your new garlic where last year's was kept until you have cleaned out all the debris and washed the area well.

Canker and Mildew

These are a problem of wet soil — either the soil is badly drained, or you've overwatered, or it's rained too much. Alternatively, there may be undecomposed organic matter in the soil surrounding the bulb, which stays wet when the soil is almost dry.

HARVESTING GARLIC

Garlic is good to chew and fumigate.

~

AN ASSYRIAN HERBAL, 8TH CENTURY BC

Garlic takes between five and nine months (depending on climate
and variety) to mature. Once the flower dies and the stalk begins to
wither, it is time for you to harvest the garlic. Don't wait for the stalk
and leaves to completely wither, as you would with onions — pull up
the stalk when it's leathery and yellowing.

Garlic can be pulled up by hand when in soft, moist soil — but soft,
moist soil tends to stick to the bulb. It's best to wait for a dry period
and fork carefully under the plant, gently break up the soil, then pull.

Once your garlic is above ground, brush off all the dirt, or leave it to
dry for an hour or so until it can be scraped off. Don't wait any longer or
you will get dirt-stained leaves. Now peel off all the 'dirty' bits of skin
until you're left with white — or purple or pink, but at any rate
CLEAN — garlic. Garlic can be bleached, and commercial garlic often
is, but there is no need when it is for home use. I much prefer garlic's
natural cream, green or purple colours to pristine whiteness.

Leave the garlic — and its stalk if you want to braid it — on racks in
a dry place for a few weeks. This is to dry out the leaves — usually the
stalk dries quite well by itself, as moisture is drawn into the bulb or the

seed head, but the leaves can turn black and mouldy quickly. If that happens, infection can travel down to the bulb — leaving no stalk or leaves for braiding — if you don't cut it off as soon as possible.

When the leaves are quite papery, you can either hang the garlic in bags, braid them, knot them together, simply let them hang in bunches, or leave them on the racks until you need them. Remember to keep some of your garlic so that you can plant it again ... and again ... and again. You will gradually develop a cultivar suited to your area and your gardening habits.

WHAT HAPPENS IF YOU DON'T HARVEST YOUR GARLIC

Most of my garlic never gets properly harvested. Whenever I find a new source of cloves, I plant a few, to see which grow best or differently from the ones I already have. Some of them get pulled up; some get used as 'garlic leeks'; the green bits of some are snipped for salads.

But most are just left to multiply.

And multiply they do. I now have great clumps of garlic under the trees and at the edges of my garden beds. The clumps get bigger every year while the stems get smaller — the bulbs below ground are possibly getting smaller too. But the stems are still tender and the leaves delicately garlic-flavoured. If you want a low-maintenance source of 'garlic leeks', this is the best way of doing it — plant the cloves and forget them until you want to harvest a few stems.

COOKING WITH GARLIC

Do not eat garlic or onions; for their smell will reveal that you are a peasant.

~

CERVANTES, DON QUIXOTE, 1614

Garlic has two quite distinct flavours, raw and cooked. But within these two flavours, there are many subtle nuances and variations.

Cooked garlic is sweetest when it is fried lightly before using — just enough to soften it slightly without browning or burning. Garlic that is cooked for a long time without this preliminary frying can become slightly bitter — not enough to taint the dish, but enough to make a difference to a sensitive palate. (This doesn't apply to quickly cooked dishes like garlic bread, where the garlic is barely heated through, or to meats such as mutton or chicken spiced with garlic — the garlic is cooked naturally in the fat from the meat.)

A traditional method of cooking garlic to relieve its acridity was to simmer it in a small quantity of rich stock or milk.

The flavour of raw garlic can also vary. Garlic rubbed around a wooden salad bowl tastes faint and

Roast Chicken with Garlic

❧

SERVES 4

Simply place a layer of peeled garlic cloves under a chicken, along with plenty of butter and perhaps a few sprigs of tarragon. Cook the chicken slowly — this isn't a recipe for a small bird — so the garlic cooks without hardening in the fat and the chicken juices, and becomes rich and caramelised.

This dish is even better if you can use immature, whole garlic bulbs rather than mature garlic cloves. The immature garlic is tender, rich and not nearly as pungent.

Lamb and Garlic Kebabs

SERVES 4

~ 1 kg (2 lb) lamb, cut into chunks
~ juice of 2 lemons
~ 1 tbspn olive oil
~ 12 garlic cloves
~ 1 tspn chopped white onion (optional)
~ 1 tspn fresh parsley, finely chopped
~ 2 cups (500 ml/16 fl oz) natural (plain) yogurt
~ ½ tspn paprika

Marinate the lamb in the lemon juice, oil, half the garlic (which has been chopped), the onion and the parsley for at least 3 hours. (I've marinated it for up to a week in a cool place — it was delicious.) Remove the lamb from the marinade, thread onto skewers and grill over a HOT fire — the meat should be singed outside but pink inside.

Crush the remaining garlic and mix into the yoghurt. As each skewer is cooked, ladle a little of the yoghurt over it and dust with paprika. Serve hot with thick chunks of crusty white bread or pita bread.

acrid. But if it is smeared over an unglazed pottery dish which is then filled with a chicken to be roasted or potatoes in cream, or some other fatty food, it can give a wonderfully rich but elusive aroma.

Garlic may be added to a dish not only to flavour it, but also to tenderise the meat (especially old mutton), or to thicken the juices.

Often, well-cooked, fatty dishes with enormous amounts of garlic will taste less garlicky than dishes with small amounts of garlic but with more fluid and less fat. One clove in a bottle of homemade tomato sauce, for example, gives a strong, pungent flavour, while 20 cloves with a roast chicken gives a creamy richness.

Only fresh, firm, white or creamy garlic should be used. Avoid any that looks mouldy or brown, as the flavour may be harsh or even unpleasant. In some recipes the green centre of the garlic clove is cut out. In most cases it is a good idea to cut away the tough base unless you are using a garlic crusher.

How to Use a Garlic Clove

Crushed

Stick a garlic clove in a garlic crusher. There is no need to peel it. Crush it and use the garlicky ooze that comes out through the end.

Crushed garlic is perhaps the most convenient way of preparing garlic (though you do have to wash the crusher, which is fiddly), but the contact between the metal and the raw garlic seems to give a sharp, acrid flavour. You can now find stainless steel garlic crushers that have a black, heavy-duty nylon or plastic basket where the garlic bulbs are inserted, thus minimising the problem of strange metallic flavours — they are worth hunting out.

Garlic Oil

The traditional method of making herb oils gives an acid after-taste when used to make garlic oil. This recipe gives a much better result and is good with salads or for dripping on toast. It isn't suitable for cooking.

Peel 12 garlic cloves, throw them in boiling water and leave for 3 minutes. Scoop them out.

Crush them with the back of a spoon — don't use a garlic crusher as the result will be bitter. Cover with 2 cups (500 ml/16 fl oz) oil. Leave for 10 minutes, then strain well through muslin (cheesecloth) or a very fine sieve. Bottle the strained oil and seal well. Keep in a cool, dark place until needed.

Garlic Stems in Olive Oil

Splash some olive oil into a saucepan, then add the garlic stems, trimmed of their tough top and outer leaves. You can add a few chopped, skinned tomatoes or slices of capsicum (sweet pepper), but all you really need is the stem and olive oil.

Cover the saucepan, put it on top of the stove or in the oven and cook slowly for about 2 hours. Drizzle with lemon or lime juice, add pepper if you like, and eat it with whole new potatoes or fresh baked bread.

Garlic and Chilli Relish

~ 20 garlic cloves
~ 4 fresh red chillies
~ juice of 1 lime (use lemon only if absolutely necessary)
~ 1 thspn brown (demerara) sugar
~ 1 cup (250 ml/8 fl oz) coconut milk

Chop the garlic and chillies roughly. Add the other ingredients and simmer until thick. Store in small, clean bottles in the refrigerator.

Squashed

Place a clove on a hard surface and squash it with the back of a knife or a heavy spoon. There is no need to peel the clove as the skin is easily removed after squashing.

Bruised

Bruised garlic is perhaps best in a salad dressing. Squash the clove enough to let the flavour permeate the dressing. It is then easy to avoid eating the whole cloves, or to seek them out — garlic enthusiasts can crunch on them, delicately flavoured with dressing.

Sliced

I believe this preserves the flavour of garlic better than crushing or squashing. Hold the garlic at the narrow end and, with a very sharp knife, slice down almost to the base in a series of parallel lines. Turn the clove 90 degrees and repeat. Then slice across the top of the bulb horizontally until you have reduced the entire clove to miniature dice.

Whole

In long-stewing or -roasting dishes, garlic is best left whole. If you want it to thicken the dish — whole garlic will gradually help thicken a sauce or gravy — or you plan to eat the whole cloves, peel them first. If you just want the flavour — especially with roast meat — place the cloves whole and unpeeled near the roast, then remove them when cooking is finished. The cloves may be hard and crisp by then, but their flavour will linger amongst the meat and juices.

USING THE OTHER PARTS OF GARLIC

The traditional way of consuming garlic is of course to eat the peeled cloves. But other parts of garlic are also good.

'Garlic Leeks' or Stems

These are the immature leaves and stem of the plant that appear before the stalk. They can be used at any time, and are delicious — as tender as normal leeks but delicately garlicky.

Garlic Flower Stems

Old garlic flower stems are dry or tough. New ones are tender and crisp. Sometimes a moderately old stem seems tough, but is still good if peeled. Garlic stems can be thinly sliced and eaten with salads or as part of an antipasto with mayonnaise. They are lovely stir-fried or added to stews. They taste very mildly of garlic.

Garlic Leaves

If you don't have any garlic bulbs on hand, snip off a few garlic leaves, chop them well and add them to salads and stews instead. They are best used raw or added in the last few minutes of cooking because they lose their flavour when cooked for a while. They make an excellent salad green, especially when young and tender in early spring.

Dried Garlic

Peel your garlic cloves and dry them very slowly in the oven. When they are dry, purée them in a blender (liquidiser) or pound them in a mortar, then dry the sticky paste in the oven. Blend or pound again. This should now form a chunky powder. Press the powder through a sieve and store in clean, dry jars with a few grains of rice to soak up any moisture. If well sealed, dried garlic lasts for months — but the seal must be perfect or the powder will become lumpy and sometimes smelly.

Garlic Flowers

A few added to a salad at the last minute (so they don't discolour in the dressing) give a nice crunch.

Immature Garlic

This is my favourite way of eating garlic. Pull up the immature plant before the flower appears. The garlic won't have formed cloves — it will still be one solid 'round', like an onion. It will be garlicky, tender, not as pungent as mature garlic, but sweet and almost indescribable. Eat it thinly sliced in salads, sliced then dipped in batter and deep-fried, added to stir-fried dishes instead of onions, or use to thicken stews. Any of the garlic recipes in this book can also be cooked using immature garlic.

PRESERVED GARLIC

Garlic is the ultimate natural convenience food, perfectly packaged when you pull it from the ground. A garlic garland will last at least a year — by which time you will have fresh garlic again.

NO artificially preserved garlic tastes like fresh garlic. Most methods of preserving garlic accentuate the rotten-egg smell — you get pungency without flavour. So where you can, use garlic fresh — it only takes a little bit longer to push an unpeeled clove through the garlic crusher, or to chop it with a knife, than it takes to open a jar. And NEVER try to make herb oils or vinegars with garlic — you'll spoil the taste of the oils, the vinegars, the herbs and the garlic.

There are some good ways of conserving garlic, rather than preserving it. The flavour is not the same as fresh garlic, but it is still acceptable. Try some of the recipes for pickling, drying, or making oils and relishes (pages 27–31). In an attractive jar or container, they also make good presents.

This is perhaps the best of the garlic conserves — not only a way of keeping garlic, but a dish in itself, a good garnish for fried rice or noodles, or tossed into salads rich with meat or fish.

~ *6 garlic bulbs*

~ *1 cup (250 g/8 oz) sugar*

~ *1 cup (250 ml/8 fl oz) (distilled) white vinegar*

~ *1 cup (250 ml/8 fl oz) water*

Separate the garlic into cloves and peel each one. Cut off the tough bases.

Simmer the sugar, vinegar and water for 20 minutes. Drop in the garlic and bring to the boil. Take off the heat at once. Pour hot into clean jars and seal. Keep in a cool, dark place for at least a week before using. Pickled garlic will last for several months, but keep the jar in the refrigerator once opened.

Garlic Salad Basket

~ 4 garlic cloves, crushed
~ 60 g (2 oz) butter or
¼ cup (60 ml/2 fl oz)
olive oil
~ stale bread, sliced

Add the garlic to the butter
or oil and heat until the
butter is melted or the oil is
just starting to smoke. Take
it off the heat at once.

Brush both sides of the
bread with the garlic-
flavoured butter or oil. Place
in a patty cake tin (muffin
pan) or any other tin that
will keep the bread in a
basket shape as it cooks.
Bake in a moderate oven
until brown.

These garlic baskets are
best used fresh, when still
slightly warm, but can be
stored in a sealed container
for a day or two. Fill them
with salad and sprinkle
with salad dressing just
before the salad is to be
eaten, or the bread will
go soggy.

GARLIC AND SALADS

The old-fashioned way of adding garlic to a salad
was to rub it around the salad bowl. This made the
bowl extremely tasty but left nothing much for the
salad. An alternative for those who didn't like
garlic overly much was to have the salad tossed by
a chef who was very fond of it. The chef breathed
on the salad and that lingering aroma was enough
to scent the salad.

Actually, the flavour — or smell — of badly
digested garlic is different to that of raw garlic in
a salad. Anyone who has ever eaten a chef-tainted
salad may well have decided that they definitely
don't want a closer garlic encounter.

MEDICINAL GARLIC

Sith garlicke then hath power to save from death,
Beare with it though it makes unsavoury breath;
And scorn not garlicke, like to some that thinke,
It only makes men winke, and drinke and stinke.

~

SIR JOHN HARRINGTON, THE ENGLISH DOCTOR, 1609

Garlic has been used medicinally for possibly almost as long as it has been cultivated. Even early this century, for example, fresh garlic juice was dripped onto wounds (painful and smelly but an effective disinfectant). It was also administered to help cure colds, asthma, consumption, rheumatism and to expel worms. Garlic was chopped into molasses, or made into a syrup with sugar and vinegar, and eaten before breakfast to clear the bowels — clearing the bowels being a noted way of ensuring that the body stayed free of infection.

Garlic Antiseptic

Rub an abrasion with a freshly cut clove of garlic instead of dabbing it with a proprietary disinfectant.

Garlic Poultice

This is excellent for abrasions. You can use either garlic cloves or leaves.

Crush the garlic cloves and apply to the affected area. If using leaves, chop then boil until soft — this takes about 2–3 minutes. Alternatively, purée in a blender (liquidiser). The poultice should then be applied warm.

Garlic Poultice for Corns, Warts and Verrucas

Top the corn, wart or verruca with crushed garlic and keep it in place with a bandaid. Over the next few days to a week, it will soften.

Gelatin Garlic Capsules

If you don't feel you can swallow raw garlic, buy gelatin capsules from your chemist and fill them with crushed garlic. These won't keep — you will need to use them within a few hours. They can also be filled with Dried Garlic (page 30), but this may not be as effective as fresh garlic.

Homemade Garlic Capsules

Cut each clove into quarters and wrap in a little bread. Squash the bread and garlic in your fingers to reduce the size, then swallow whole with a glass of water.

Less reliably, people with infections wore fresh garlic cloves inside their stockings during the day and in their bedsocks at night for two weeks.

Flaking skin on the bottom of the feet was supposed to show that the garlic had drawn the infection out of the body. A 19th century recipe (possibly older) recommended applying a paste of garlic and sour milk to the chest to help with respiratory problems and bronchitis, and a paste of garlic and vinegar on brown paper, reapplied every hour, was used as a cure for diphtheria.

In recent decades, research has shown garlic to be effective in a range of medical applications, from helping in the treatment of heart disease to inhibiting the growth of tumours, inhibiting viruses, and lowering blood pressure and blood sugar levels, to being used as a simple disinfectant for a cut finger or pimples. Given the potency of garlic against so many ailments, it might be wondered why it hasn't been used more often in conventional medicine.

The answer isn't simply because of its smell — nor is it because large companies prefer drugs that can be patented or synthesised. The main reason for garlic's lack of use in conventional medicine is that the active ingredient in garlic, allicin, is relatively indiscriminate — it can just as easily kill or harm human cells as those of dangerous micro-organisms. It is also extremely unstable. Most processed garlic is far less active than fresh garlic. In addition, it is short-lived, with a chemical half-life of two to four hours at room temperature.

Garlic, therefore, should usually be eaten raw and fresh to be most effective. (In some applications, however, cooked garlic is as effective as, or even more effective than, raw garlic — notably in reducing cholesterol and blood-clotting.)

HOW TO TAKE MEDICINAL GARLIC

As I've already said, to get the best results, medicinal garlic should usually be eaten raw. If you baulk at the idea of raw garlic, you could always try the commercial garlic tablets and capsules that are available in many forms at health food stores and supermarkets. Garlic is also added to many other herbal medicines. The less these preparations smell of garlic, however, the less effective they are likely to be — there is no such thing as odour-free and effective garlic. The effectiveness of these commercial garlic products can vary enormously.

Garlic can also be taken as part of a drink, by blending it with fruit juice — orange or pineapple juice is good — or milk. This makes a relatively unpleasant drink, but it is still more palatable than chewing raw garlic.

Garlic Sandwich

Butter a slice of bread well and cover with chopped or crushed garlic. Try not to chew too much — you want the bread to surround the garlic for as long as possible. A friend adds Vegemite or Marmite to his garlic sandwiches. He says it kills the taste. I think it makes it worse.

An even better garlic sandwich involves spreading a thick layer of cream, cottage or other cheese on the bread before adding the garlic.

Garlic Mixture for Arthritis

Garlic steeped in olive oil, then warmed and rubbed into inflamed areas, is an old gypsy treatment for arthritis and rheumatism. The recipe below is also reputed to give some relief.

Fill a jar with chopped garlic (don't bother to peel it). Add enough vodka (or whisky, rum or brandy) to cover. Leave in a warm, dark place for a month. Take ½ tspn before meals.

If you want to avoid the alcohol, place ½ tspn of the mixture in a saucer and add ½ cup (125 ml/4 fl oz) boiling water (this should evaporate most of the alcohol). Let it cool before you drink it.

A good, safe, home-prescribed garlic dose would be no more than one to two raw cloves a day, taken with other food. Because raw garlic can irritate the stomach, small doses with meals are the best way of avoiding indigestion. If you are going to eat a couple of salads with raw garlic in them, for example, don't eat any other raw garlic that day.

Alternatively, you could eat one massively garlicky meal or several meals with not so much garlic — but only if the garlic has been cooked.

As a general rule, any culinary use and the occasional larger dose of garlic are safe. It is only where very large amounts are regularly taken for medicinal purposes that problems may arise — e.g. inflammation of the digestive tract, chronic indigestion, vomiting or diarrhoea. Extremely large amounts — such as 30 g (1 oz) per day — have been associated with anaemia and the deformation of red blood cells. Large amounts should only be taken with the knowledge of an experienced medical practitioner.

During pregnancy, avoid eating large quantities of garlic and using garlic medicinally. It may cause heartburn, and as a general precaution, no substance should be taken in large amounts in the early months of pregnancy. Eating large amounts of garlic while breast-feeding may give the milk a garlic flavour — which may or may not be appreciated by the baby.

Note: The remedies that I suggest may be effective, but don't rely on them. ALL medical conditions should be diagnosed and treated by a qualified general practitioner — and ALL herbal remedies contain active ingredients that may conflict with treatments you are already taking. If you wish to add these to your treatment, discuss them with your doctor first. (If, however, the doctor sniggers at the idea of medicinal herbs, you might consider finding another doctor.)

ANTI-VIRAL GARLIC

Fresh garlic will suppress several common viruses, including herpes simplex, human rhinovirus 2, and para-influenza type 3. However, steamed, distilled and oil-macerated garlic products were shown to have no effect in various trials, nor did dried garlic or old, crushed garlic. Most commercial garlic products appeared to be extremely variable in their effect on the viruses tested.

Kick-A-Germ Juice

This is a traditional kill or cure anti-cold treatment. It is one of the most disgusting drinks invented. Its chief advantage may be that it makes you feel so terrible, you have to go to bed.

Combine 2 chopped or crushed garlic cloves, juice of 2 lemons or limes, 1 tspn powdered or grated, fresh ginger, ½ chilli, chopped, or 2–3 drops of Tabasco sauce, and 1 cup (250 ml/8 fl oz) hot water. Drink FAST. (Few people are able to drink it slowly.) Then go to bed. If you experience side effects, don't say I didn't warn you.

Garlic Candies

SERVES 4

These are surprisingly good — crisp on the outside, soft on the inside, and sweet and pungent.

~ 1 cup (250 g/8 oz) sugar

~ 1 cup (250 ml/8 fl oz) water

~ 20–40 garlic cloves

~ 2 tspns poppy seeds

~ 2 tspns sesame seeds, roasted or browned in a little oil

Simmer the sugar and water for about 10 minutes or until a little of the syrup just sets in a saucer of water. Add the garlic and simmer for 5 minutes. Scoop the garlic out of the syrup and leave to dry on greased baking trays (sheets). When they are nearly dry but still tacky, roll them in the poppy and sesame seeds. Store in a very dry jar between layers of greaseproof (wax) paper — but because they will soften after a day or two, they are best eaten within a few hours.

GARLIC, INFECTIONS AND THE IMMUNE SYSTEM

Garlic may act as an immunostimulant, building up resistance to infections. Taking four to five raw garlic cloves a day is said to help ease thrush, skin problems, respiratory disorders and many other persistent infections — this treatment should be undertaken only under medical supervision. Eating garlic regularly may also help prevent infections, and it has been said to help ward off colds, influenza, and decrease herpes attacks.

Large amounts of raw or cooked garlic may help reduce the incidence of stomach cancer. It has also been found to activate the liver to destroy the aflatoxin that is found on mouldy peanuts, which can trigger liver cancer. It may help protect against some of the effects of smoked and barbecued meat. In a 12-week German study into the effects of garlic on people with AIDS, the incidence of diarrhoea, candida, sinusitis and recurrent fever decreased, and there were other indications of immune-system improvement in six of the ten patients. (Three withdrew due to digestive problems.)

GARLIC AND THRUSH

Garlic is an effective anti-fungal agent, and a strong solution of fresh garlic and water may be used as a douche against vaginal thrush. Equally effective remedies, however, are also available, and the long-term effects of douching with garlic have not been tested. (It is worth remembering, of course, that every effective treatment probably has side effects.)

GARLIC AND HEART DISEASE

Eating raw or cooked garlic (preferably both) regularly may reduce the risk of heart attack or of further heart attacks. At least 1 g, preferably 2 g, of dried garlic or 5 g of fresh garlic need to be taken every day to be effective. However, the exact minimum effective dose may depend on body weight and various other factors — even small amounts may have some effect.

Research has indicated that regular consumption of large amounts of garlic may reduce cholesterol levels. Triglycerides and blood-clotting tendencies may also be reduced. The effect on blood-clotting is greater if cooked garlic is taken — because of its high ajeone content — rather than raw garlic or garlic preparations. Cooked garlic also retains most of its anti-cholesterol activity.

GARLIC AND LATE-ONSET DIABETES

Garlic may help to lower blood sugar levels, and has been used by herbalists in the treatment of late-onset diabetes. Four to six fresh cloves a day should be taken — but again, only under medical supervision.

GARLIC AND POLLUTION

Animals with high levels of heavy-metal poisoning showed a higher than normal survival rate when fed large amounts of garlic.

Garlic and Pistachio Soufflé

SERVES 4

~ 1 tbspn butter

~ 6 garlic cloves

~ 2 cups (500 ml/16 fl oz) (single/light) cream

~ ½ cup (60 g/2 oz) ground pistachios

~ 5 eggs, separated

Melt the butter and cook the garlic slowly, until it is soft. Don't burn or brown. Mash the garlic and butter together, take off the heat, and stir in the cream, pistachios and egg yolks.

Whip the egg whites (preferably in a copper bowl) until stiff, then gently fold in the pistachio mixture. Pour into an unbuttered soufflé or baking dish. Cook in a preheated hot oven (about 250°C/500°F/Gas Mark 9) for about 20 minutes or until it rises and is brown. (Exact cooking times depend on the size and shape of the dish.) Don't overcook — the top should be golden, not leathery. Serve hot.

GARLIC AND SEX

Eat no onions or garlic, for we are to utter sweet breath.

~

WILLIAM SHAKESPEARE, A MIDSUMMER NIGHT'S DREAM, 1600

Garlic's reputation for increasing strength did not limit its application to the building of pyramids or the waging of wars. Pliny, the Ancient Greek writer, recommended crushed garlic and coriander (cilantro) in white wine as a sexual stimulant. Presumably this is only effective if both partners partake, or if the partner who does not has a cold.

On the other hand, rats fed garlic over a long period of time had lowered blood sugar levels and cholesterol, but they also experienced lower sperm production and, eventually, testicular lesions. The amount they were fed, however, was equivalent to about 20 g (¾ oz) of garlic powder a day for an average human — an enormous quantity. The average garlic-eating lover has nothing to worry about.

COSMETIC GARLIC

Eating lots of garlic is said to be good for clear, blemish-free skin. It can also be mixed into a range of concoctions and applied directly to the skin, with beneficial results.

Garlic Cleanser for Spotty Complexions

Place 1 cup (60 g/2 oz) chopped lavender flowers in a jar. Add 10 chopped garlic cloves and top with boiling vinegar. Seal when cool and keep in the refrigerator. Apply a little of this lotion with cotton wool to clean your face in the morning. Let it dry on the skin before washing off.

Garlic and Lemon Face Mask for Oily Skin and Blackheads

Crush garlic and stir it into an equal amount of lemon juice. Wipe the mask over your face, then cover with a hot, wet towel. (This can be heated in the oven or a microwave, but make sure it is not too hot.) Leave the towel on until it has cooled. Wash your face in cold water, then in warm soapy water to remove the smell.

Garlic Spray

*Chop your garlic well —
there is no need to peel it.
Place it in a glass jar (don't
leave it in metal as it may
react) and only just cover
with mineral oil. Leave
overnight.*

*Strain the next day (or
whenever you need to use it)
and dilute with 20 parts
water for every 1 part of
garlic-impregnated oil. If
you use slightly soapy water,
the spray will 'stick' better to
the plants. Alternatively,
add 1 tspn fish emulsion for
every 4–6 cups (1–1.5 l/
1¼–2½ imp pt) water.*

GARLIC AND GARDENING

Garlic has been hailed as a pest repellent,
a pesticide, even as a fungicide.

In my own trials, however, roses with garlic
planted around them showed no resistance at all to
black spot — but they did have fewer aphids, not
because the aphids were repelled by the scent of the
garlic, but because once the garlic flowered, a range
of hover flies, tiny wasps and other pest predators
were attracted to the flowers, and their offspring
controlled the aphids. Planting garlic around peach
trees is also believed to inhibit curly leaf, though
trials that I have conducted have been inconclusive
to date. A few garlic plants around a tree will have
no effect at all, but it is possible that very large
amounts will help.

Another way of using garlic in the garden is as a
spray. Garlic spray is simple to make, doesn't smell
as bad as you would think, and will keep for at least
a month if stored in a sealed container in a cool,
dark place. However, its effects are variable. While
some tests have shown it to be a potent pesticide —
especially effective against mosquito larvae, aphids
and onion flies — other tests have shown it to be
more effective as a repellent than as a pesticide. It is
possible that garlic spray is less effective in hot or

dry climates. More research needs to be done. Garlic spray can also be used as a weak fungicide. It has been used to control late blight in potatoes and tomatoes (spray every three days) and also helps control fusarium wilt in tomatoes. Impregnate the soil thoroughly with garlic spray after an infected crop, then cover with clear plastic for a month to clear the infection from the soil.

Garlic spray is effective in controlling leaf spots, such as chocolate spot on broad beans and black spot on roses. It may also be useful against mildews that breed in the sweet secretions of sap-sucking insects. It repels these pests, and has some capacity to inhibit some of the mildews.

A paste of crushed garlic will also have benefits. Spread thickly on dormant bulbs, it may speed up their sprouting, as well as deter or kill many of the pests, diseases and fungal problems that infect stored bulbs. Apply the paste to the bulbs, then keep the treated bulbs in a cool, dark place for two days before you plant them. There is no need to rub the garlic paste off before planting — it will be absorbed by the soil.

Tomato and Garlic Salad

SERVES 4

~ 8 sweet red tomatoes, sliced

~ 8 garlic cloves, bruised

~ olive oil

Arrange the tomato slices on a plate. Whip the bruised garlic and olive oil together and sprinkle over the tomatoes. Don't add vinegar or lemon juice — the tomato and the garlic will be acidic enough.

Garlic and Beetroot

SERVES 4

~ 4 beetroots (beets)

~ olive oil

~ squeeze of lemon juice

~ 4–8 garlic cloves

Steam or bake the beetroots, dress with plenty of olive oil, a good squeeze of lemon juice and some crushed, bruised or chopped garlic. Eat hot.

Garlic Pizza

SERVES 4

Yes, this recipe is correct — there is no cheese in what is a fragrant and very good pizza.

~ *½ cup (125 ml/4 fl oz) olive oil*

~ *2 white onions, chopped*

~ *8 garlic cloves, chopped*

~ *4 small pizza bases*

~ *½ cup (75 g/2½ oz) black olives*

~ *8–16 anchovies*

Heat the oil and cook the onion and garlic slowly until soft and almost like a thick purée. Spread over the pizza bases, then arrange the olives and anchovies on top. Place in a very hot oven and bake until the base is brown on the bottom. Serve very hot.

GARLIC AND HOUSEHOLD PESTS

Store dried garlic cloves (there is no need to peel them) with dried beans or grains to repel weevils. The dried garlic won't affect the food, although the container will smell slightly when you take the lid off. Dried garlic cloves spread along bookshelves will also repel silverfish. Bear in mind, however, that there are more attractive repellents, such as lavender, which are just as effective.

Garlands of garlic can be hung on hat racks or in cupboards to repel clothes moths — again, other pest repellents, like lavender, cloves and oranges, may smell sweeter.

GARLIC AND ANIMALS

Many wild and domestic animals will feed on garlic — I once watched a gourmet wallaby taking alternate bites of garlic leaf and lettuce. And gorillas and various other primates have been noted browsing on wild garlic. Wild garlic can, however, be a pest if dairy cattle eat it, as it can taint the taste of their milk.

Large amounts of garlic (both the leaves and bulbs) have been fed to stock both to treat and to prevent worm infestation. It is fed to animals as a general tonic, to ease mastitis, to improve the performance of stallions and bulls, and to help cure fevers and other illnesses. The medicinal garlic recipes for humans (pages 33–35) can also be used for many animals.

Garlic is usually fed to stock chopped up in bran and moistened with molasses (black treacle) to disguise the taste — animals prefer the leaves to the strong but more medicinally active cloves.

Feeding garlic regularly to cats and dogs is said to help repel ticks and fleas. Approximately one clove per day is the normal dose for medium-sized dogs, two cloves for very large dogs, and one-quarter of a clove for cats.

Grilled Eggplant with Garlic

SERVES 4

~ 2 medium eggplants (aubergines)
~ salt
~ 4 garlic cloves, finely chopped
~ a little fresh chilli (optional)
~ ½ cup (125 ml/4 fl oz) olive oil
~ 2 tbspns red wine or balsamic vinegar

Cut eggplant into slices and sprinkle with salt. Leave for 1 hour so that it loses the bitter juices, then wash in cold water. Dry well.

Place the garlic, chilli (if using) and oil in a frying pan (skillet) and heat gently for 5 minutes. Fry the eggplant slices on both sides until golden-brown, remove from the pan and sprinkle with vinegar. They can be eaten tepid or kept for up to 3 days and eaten cold as part of a platter of antipasto.

Note: Zucchini (courgettes) can be cooked in the same way, but don't need salting. Dress them with either balsamic vinegar or a little white (distilled) vinegar and shredded mint.

GIFTS FROM GARLIC

GARLIC GARLANDS

These make wonderful gifts and should last from one season to the next if kept in a dry place (preferably not above the stove, where they will get steamed by every pot of boiling vegetables).

To make garlic garlands, you will need long, firm garlic tops, quite dry. Gather three together, tie them securely at the top and start plaiting. When you have made four or five turns, pull in another strand of garlic. Keep pulling in more new strands as you progress down the plait. This sounds complicated but it is quite simple once you start — though you will possibly need practice to produce neat, tight plaits and to judge how often to pull in new strands of garlic tops. Tie the end of the garlic with string or ribbon, or knot the strands.

Once you have made your garlic garland, you can sew dried chillies, sprigs of holly, dried rose hips or any other 'herbal' or seasonal decoration into it. Garlic garlands may also be sprayed with gold or silver paint to make Christmas decorations to hang from the tree or over doorways. As long as the paint only penetrates the outer, paper skin, not the inner layers, the garlic can be eaten afterwards.

GARLIC FLOWERS

Garlic flowers are spectacular, and will last well as cut flowers in a tall vase if the water is changed regularly. They also make good dried flowers — hung in a dark, well-ventilated place until dry, then sprayed with hairspray to stop them dropping. Garlic 'seed heads' can also be dried for flower arrangements.

AND FINALLY: GARLIC AND MAGIC

Wearing a bulb of garlic around your neck was once assumed to lend
you the garlic's strength — without the odour that went with eating it.
And garlic is, of course, the vampire repellent extraordinaire. I can
truthfully assert that in 20 years of gorging on garlic (I started late),
I have never yet been attacked by a vampire.
The touch of a vampire will also wither roses, which is another good
reason for growing garlic in your garden.

ACKNOWLEDGMENTS

Sherringhams Nurseries, North Ryde

~ ~ ~

PHOTOGRAPHY
Scott Cameron Photography Pty Ltd
Ivy Hansen Photography, p. 11
Bay Picture Library, pp. 15, 19

FOOD STYLIST
Lisa Hilton

COVER PHOTOGRAPHY
Ivy Hansen